My First 1000 WORDS

Consultant: Susan A. Miller, Ed.D.

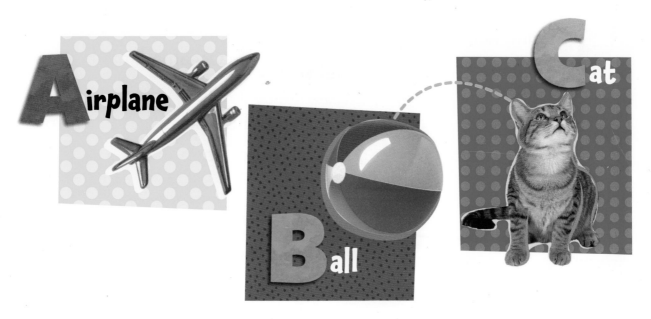

Picture credits: Adobe Systems, Inc.; Amana; Aquaware America; Artville; Brand X Pictures; Brian Warling Studios; Comstock; Cuisinart; Farberware; General Electric; Getty Images; Image Club; Kolcraft; Anna Lender; Brian Meyer; Nicholas Myers; James Mravec; Julie Risko Neely; Rachel Perrine; PhotoDisc; Rebecca Rueth; Siede Preis Photography; Rémy Simard; Stockbyte; George Ulrich; Ted Williams; © 2019 Shutterstock.

Published by Sequoia Children's Publishing,
a division of Phoenix International Publications, Inc.

8501 West Higgins Road, Suite 790
Chicago, Illinois 60631

59 Gloucester Place
London W1U 8JJ

© 2019 Sequoia Publishing & Media, LLC

www.sequoiakidsbooks.com

10 9 8 7 6 5 4 3 2 1

ISBN 978-1-64269-122-1

Contents

Get Ready to Read!

Why wait for school—give your preschooler every possible educational advantage now! Start your child down the exciting road to learning with this fantastic  book. *My First 1000 Words* is a picture/word book that helps pre-readers understand the relationship between text and speech. Read 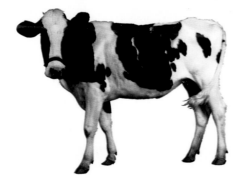 along with your child, and watch the connections form. The vocabulary words are grouped according to categories children will recognize instantly. Each word is paired with a

vibrant image to help kids connect words to people, places, and things around them.

Many categories also include sample sentences that show young readers the vocabulary words used in action. Several of these sentences contain *Dolch* sight words—common words such as *in, is,* and *it* that appear frequently in text. Vocabulary words are highlighted in blue; sight words are highlighted in red. These sample sentences demonstrate how words work together to create language. Learning these vocabulary words and seeing them used in sentences will help children begin to read with confidence and have fun doing it!

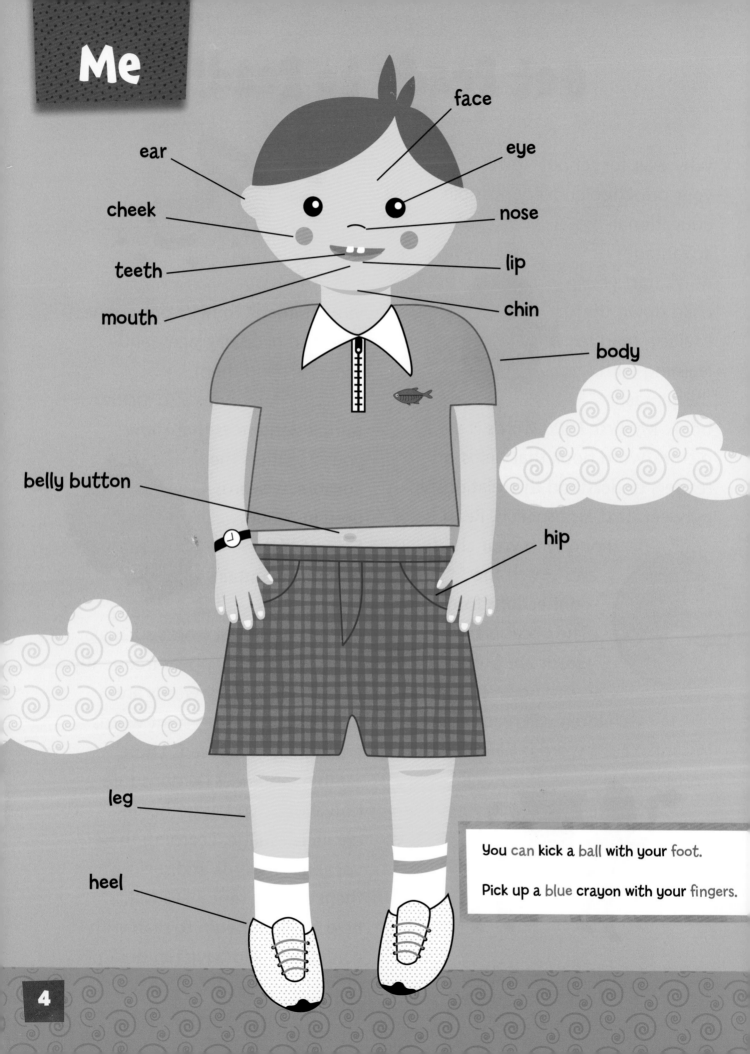

Me

face

eye

ear

nose

cheek

lip

teeth

chin

mouth

body

belly button

hip

leg

heel

You can kick a ball with your foot.

Pick up a blue crayon with your fingers.

head

hair

forehead

eyebrow

finger

hand

wrist

eyelashes

tongue

neck

shoulder

elbow

arm

back

fingernail

waist

knee

foot

ankle

toe

My Family

father   parents   mother

daughter   sister   brother   son

granddaughter   grandson

grandmother

grandfather

uncle

cousin

aunt

7

Clothes

When it rains, use an umbrella and wear a raincoat and rainboots.

The girl wore her pretty bathing suit to the beach.

sock

dress

hat

jeans

mittens

belt

glove

cap

bathing suit

vest

pajamas

shorts

skirt

shirt

apron

bonnet

underpants

jacket

snowpants

T-shirt

sunglasses

watch

zipper

button

scarf

necktie

sweater

umbrella

boots

shoes

sneakers

rainboots

flip-flops

slippers

9

My Home

chimney

house

roof

garage

window

porch

door

WELCOME

welcome mat

yard

driveway

fence

gate

mailbox

sidewalk

schoolbus

road

log cabin

hut

castle

apartment

mobile home

igloo

teepee

town house

The king and queen live in a castle.

The yellow car is parked in the garage.

The roof keeps the people who live in the house dry.

painting

lamp

vase

fireplace

table

couch

floor

telephone

candle

coffee table

Kitchen

refrigerator

salt   pepper

cupboard

cup

meal   blender   coffeemaker

dishwasher

straw

bottle

glass

high chair

chair

pot

toaster

teapot

plate dessert

microwave oven

drink

countertop

pan

kettle

stove

oven

silverware

spoon

bowl

knife

napkin

fork

table

Water is boiling in the kettle on the stove.

One egg is cooking in the pan.

The refrigerator keeps the milk cold.

Bathroom

mirror

toothbrushes

lotion

hair dryer

comb

shower

shampoo

toothpaste

soap

tissue

washcloth

sink

faucet

toilet

towels

rubber duck

bathtub

Bedroom

frame

picture

shelf

poster

closet

peace

radio

drawer

wastebasket

dresser

dress

clock

pillow

blanket

sheet

carpet

bed

nightstand

stuffed animal

All the clothes are hanging neatly in the closet.

Her mother tells her to make the bed.

Garage and Laundry

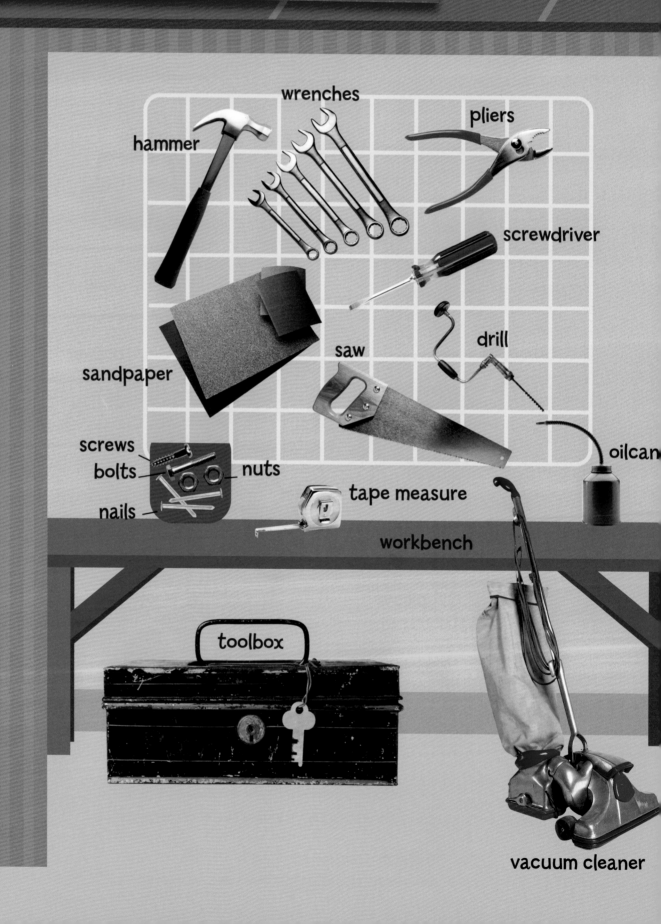

wrenches

hammer

pliers

screwdriver

sandpaper

saw

drill

oilcan

screws

bolts

nuts

nails

tape measure

workbench

toolbox

vacuum cleaner

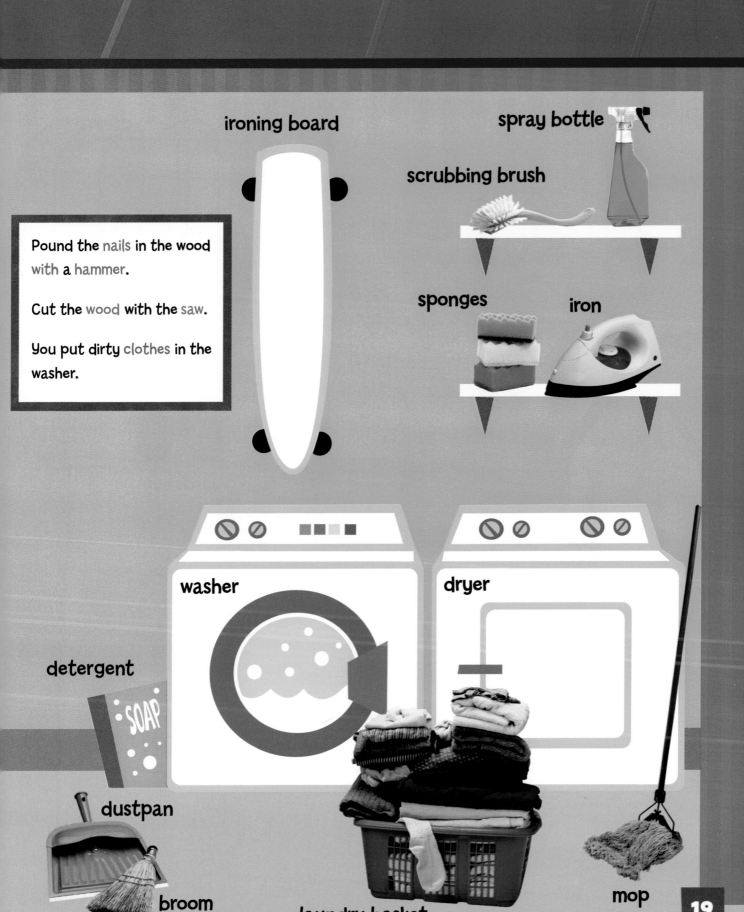

ironing board

spray bottle

scrubbing brush

Pound the nails in the wood with a hammer.

Cut the wood with the saw.

You put dirty clothes in the washer.

sponges

iron

washer

dryer

detergent

SOAP

dustpan

broom

laundry basket

mop

My Backyard

trees

greenhouse

gardener

watering can

plants

sprinkler

lawn mower

weed

lawn

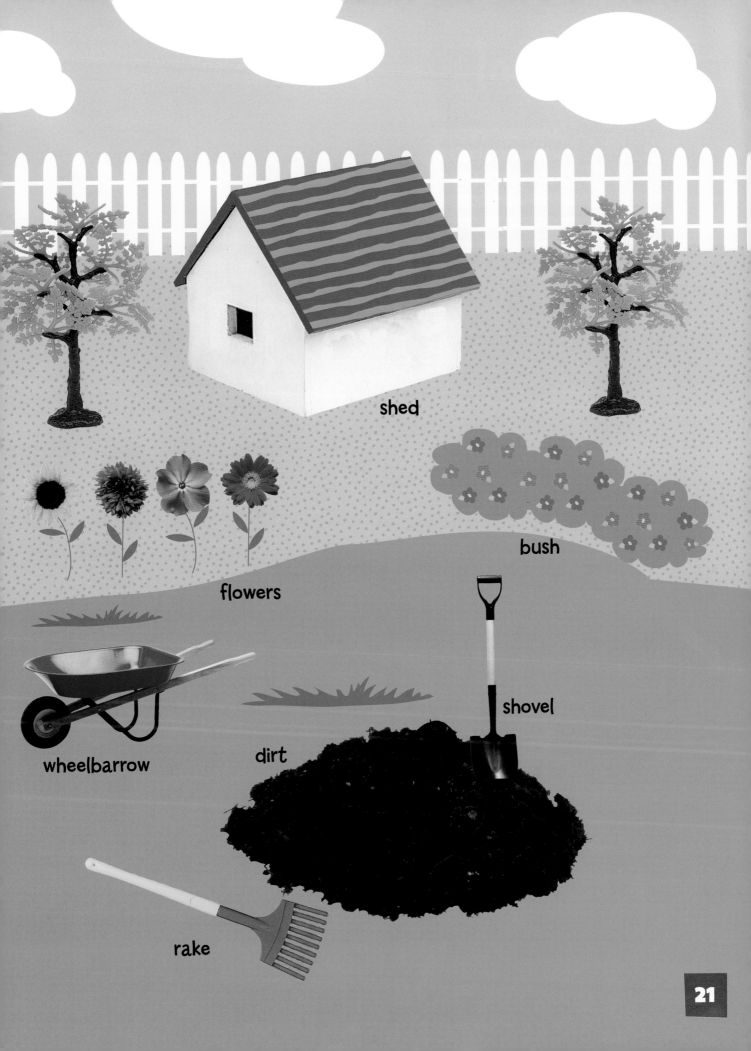

shed

bush

flowers

wheelbarrow

dirt

shovel

rake

21

My School

flag

dry-erase board

desk

lunch box

teacher

calculator

table

pen

chair

books

screen

computer

keyboard

mouse

classroom

Three friends are reading funny books together at the table.

The teacher is writing on the dry-erase board with a marker.

pencils

binders

microscope

globe

drawing

stool

paper

backpack

student

principal

Playground

kite

slide

boy

children

merry-go-round

swings

girl

jungle gym

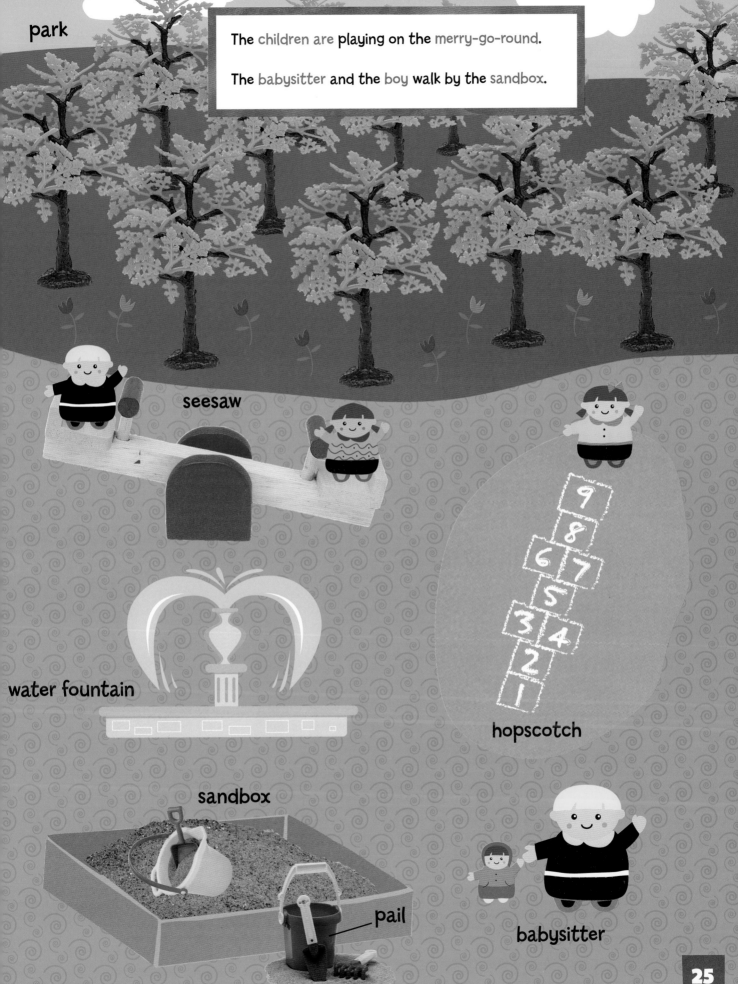

park

The children are playing on the merry-go-round.

The babysitter and the boy walk by the sandbox.

seesaw

water fountain

hopscotch

9
8
6 7
5
3 4
2
1

sandbox

pail

babysitter

25

Fire Station

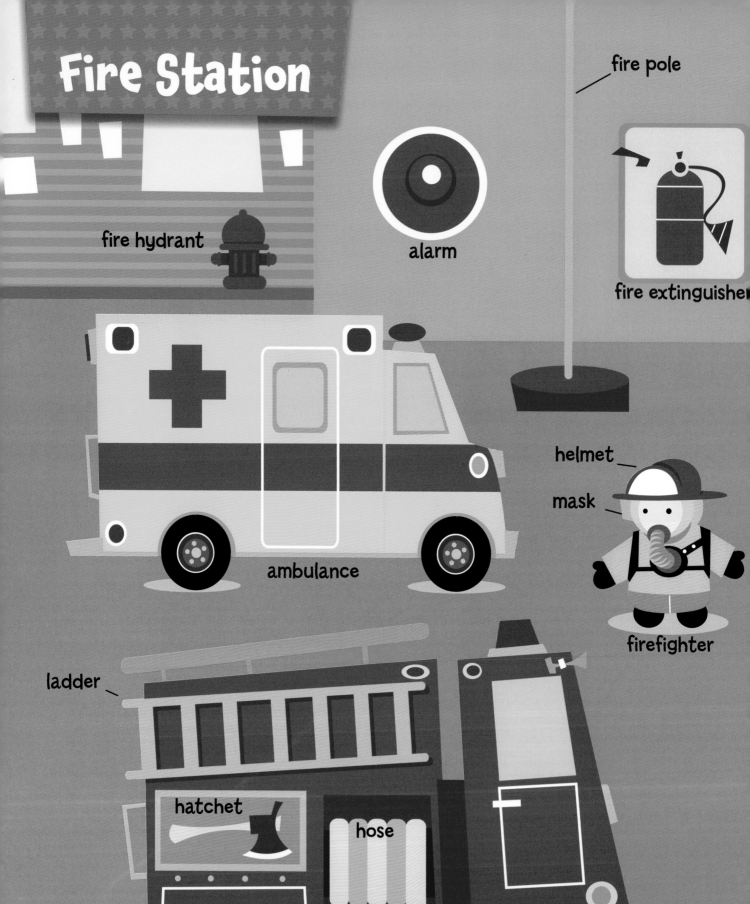

fire pole

fire hydrant

alarm

fire extinguisher

helmet

mask

firefighter

ambulance

ladder

hatchet

hose

fire truck

Police Station

POLICE

siren

police car

POLICE

uniform

badge

flashlight

motorcycle

POLICE

police officer

27

My Doctor

A patient with a broken arm will need a cast.

The nurse takes a patient's temperature with her thermometer.

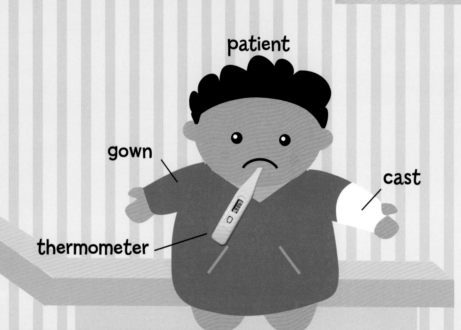

patient

gown

cast

thermometer

scale

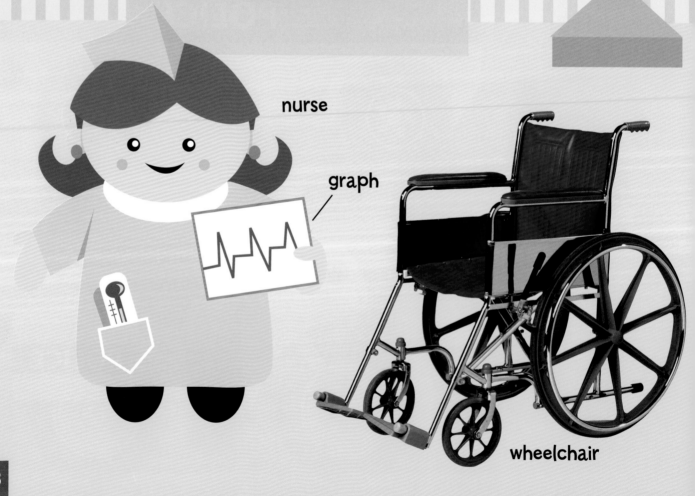

nurse

graph

wheelchair

28

crutches

medicine

bandages

Sterile
Plastic
Strips

needle

chart

doctor

stethoscope

tongue depressor

29

Supermarket

jars

cans

watermelon

FREE SAVE

coupons

pineapples

noodles

CHILI BEANS

Vegetable Broth

$1 OFF

SAVE

green beans

beets

carrots

celery

peppers

Vegetable Broth

peas

vegetables

BAKERY

baguette

baker

pitas croissant English muffin

bread

bagels

butcher

meat

fish

steak ham

cabbage

squash

potatoes

zucchini

onions

cart

fruit

grapes raspberries strawberries

cucumbers

corn blueberries cherries

31

boxes

shopper

cart

avocados

eggplants

radishes

broccoli

asparagus

spinach

lettuce

garlic

cauliflower

plums

kiwis

apricots

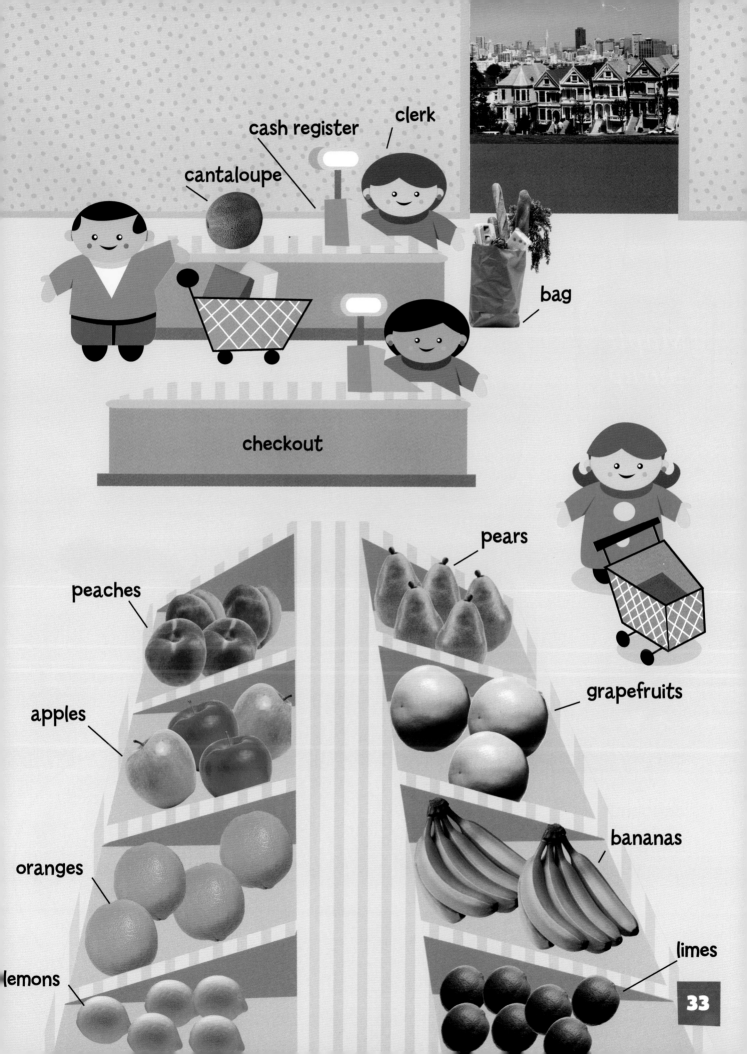

cash register

clerk

cantaloupe

bag

checkout

pears

peaches

apples

grapefruits

oranges

bananas

lemons

limes

33

Breakfast

sugar

honey

Maple Syrup

syrup

juice

tea

egg

muffin

butter

pancake

coffee

doughnut

jam

bacon

toast

sausage

cereal

Lunch

milk

bun

hamburger

macaroni

cheese

sandwich

hotdog

pickle

ketchup

mustard

tomato

roll

Pancakes, bacon, and sausage are favorite breakfast foods.

Put some ketchup on the hamburger.

soup

Dinner

spaghetti

rice

salad

chicken

pizza

water

Snacks and Dessert

yogurt

lollipop

popcorn

applesauce

cookie

ice cream

cupcake

raisins

gum balls

chips

crackers

pretzel

ice pop

chocolate

pie

Construction Site

crane

cement truck

dump truck

barrier

digger

hard hat

steamroller

worker

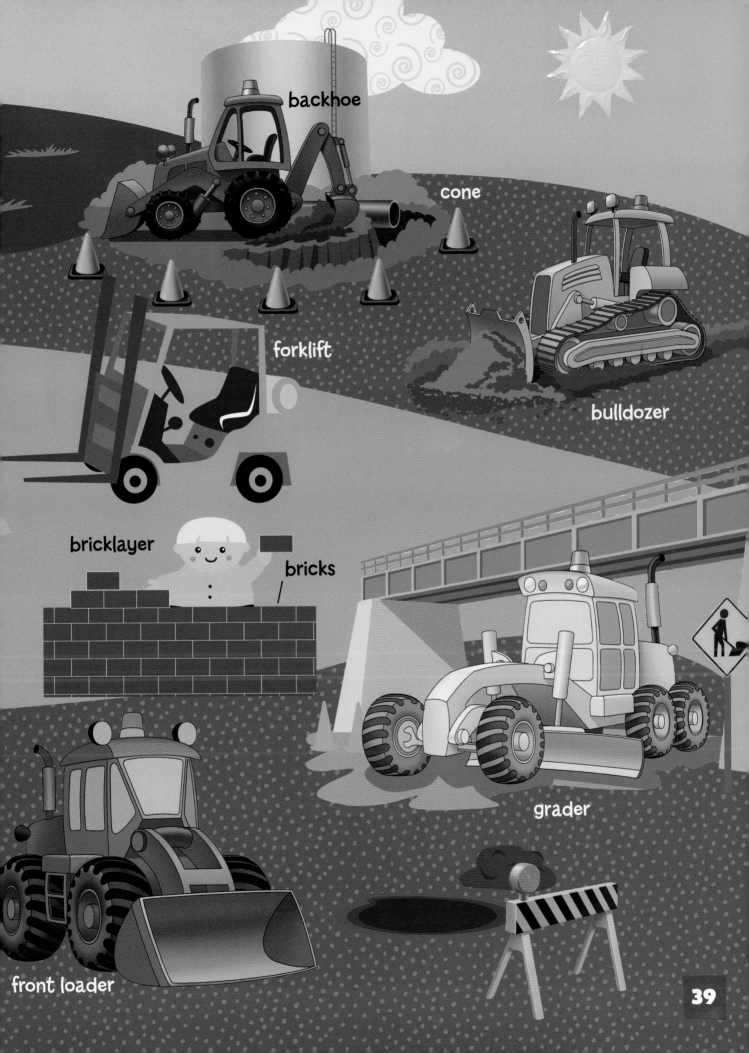

backhoe

cone

bulldozer

forklift

bricklayer

bricks

grader

front loader

39

Park

kite

bench

picnic

trash can

cooler

grass

path

camera

man

baby

woman

stroller

bicycle

lifeguard

pool

skater

diving board

skateboard

balloons

My Town

theater

SHOWTIME

Art Museum

LIBRARY

statue

church

synagogue

librarian

BANK

DRUGSTORE

Rx

laundromat

gas station

POST OFFICE

CLEAN

GARAGE

GAS

KID CARE

mechanic

$

MAIL

mailperson

day care center

The man ate a sandwich at the café next to the deli.

The bus stops for the traffic light by the bus stop.

HOTEL

HOTEL

BUS STOP

NEWS

bus driver

newsstand

bus

traffic light

restaurant

CAFÉ

DELI

FLORIST

department store

STORE

DENTIST

DINER

salesperson

STOP

stop sign

43

At Work

clown

artist

coach

ballerina

mechanic

athlete

chef

server

housekeeper

44

movers

painter

musician

carpenter

pilot

scientist

manager

Flowers

rose

sunflower

petal

leaf

thorn

stem

seeds

roots

daffodil
carnation

violet
daisy

iris
hyacinth

pansy
tulip

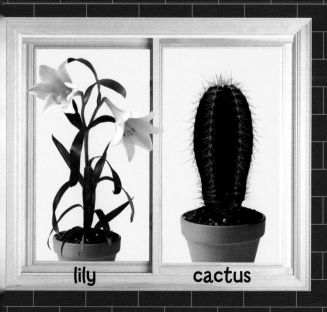

lily
cactus

lilac
orchid

47

Trees

pine tree

apple tree

trunk

pinecones

maple tree

palm tree

birch tree

coconut

oak tree

branch

bark _____

acorns

On the Farm

field

silo

barn

horse

pig

sheep

farmer

turkey

donkey

chick

hen

rooster

goat

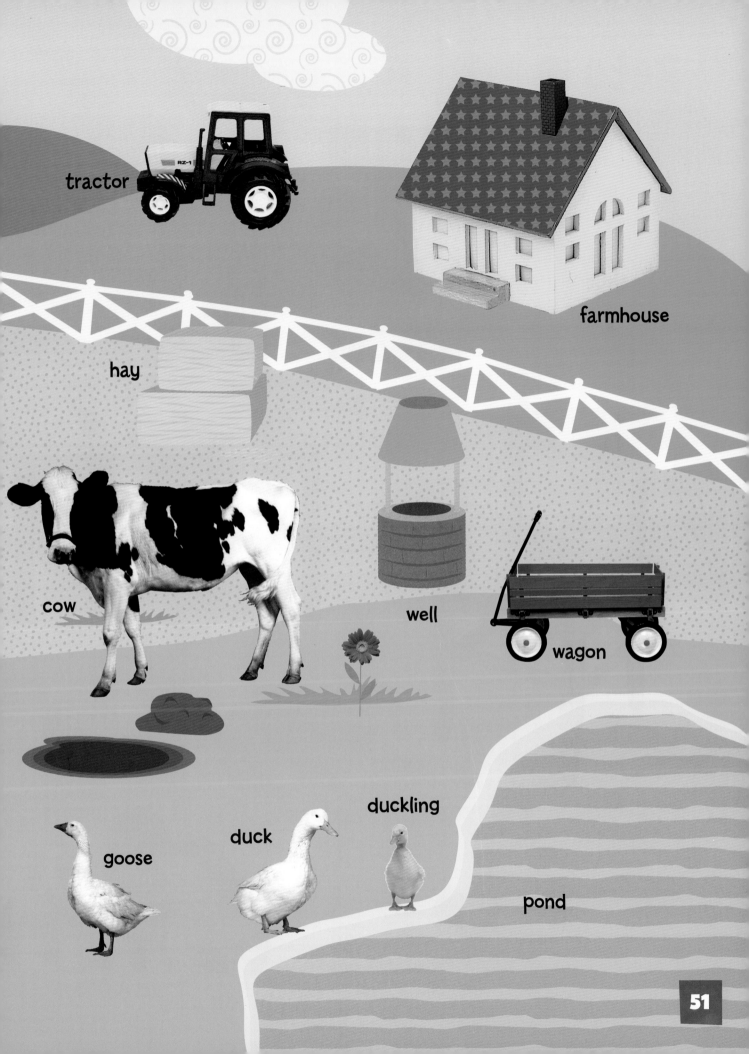

tractor

farmhouse

hay

cow

well

wagon

goose

duck

duckling

pond

51

Pets

parakeet

parrot

cat

goldfish

snail

iguana

shell

turtle

rabbit

puppies

guinea pig

pony

kittens

dog

collar

hamster

leash

ferret

Wild Animals

cheetah

_mane

lion

kangaroo

giraffe

quills

porcupine

rhinoceros

horns

alligator

bear

tusks

elephant

zebra

panda

fox

antlers

squirrel

wolf

deer

snake

monkey

skunk

raccoon

tiger

mouse

chipmunk

55

Ocean Animals

jellyfish

killer whale

fin

shark

gills

clown fish

octopus

tentacle

dolphin

seal

sea horses

fish

claw

lobster

starfish

Birds

nest

owl

swans

wing

pigeon

robin

feathers

penguin

hummingbird

flamingo

crow

dove

bluebird

beak

eagle

emu

peacock

Bugs and Insects

butterfly

moth

ladybugs

bee

ants

dragonfly

spider

web

fly

mosquito

caterpillar

cocoon

grasshopper

Transportation

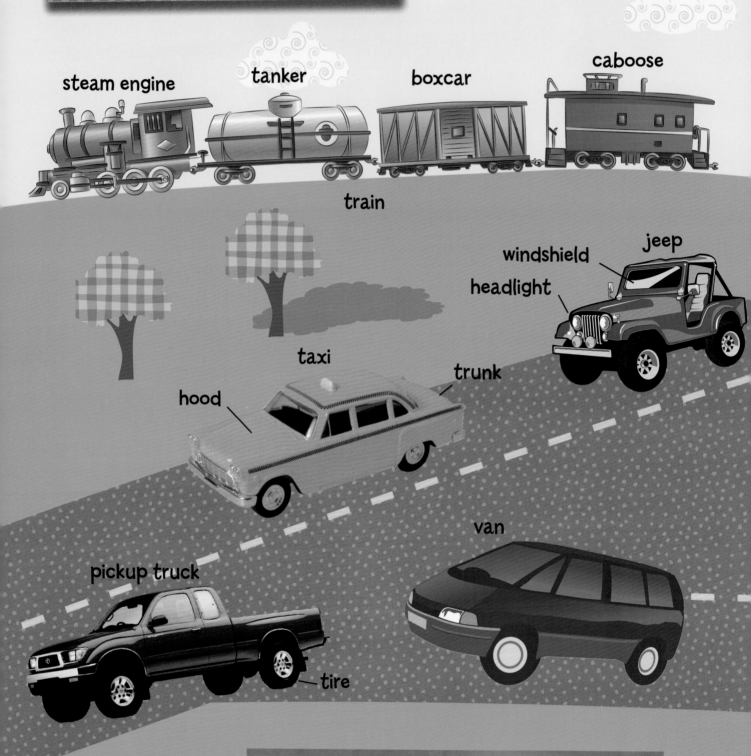

steam engine

tanker

boxcar

caboose

train

windshield

headlight

jeep

taxi

trunk

hood

van

pickup truck

tire

The top of the red convertible can go up and down.

People ride to the airport in a taxi.

station wagon

convertible

limousine

antenna

tow truck

bumper

car

wheel

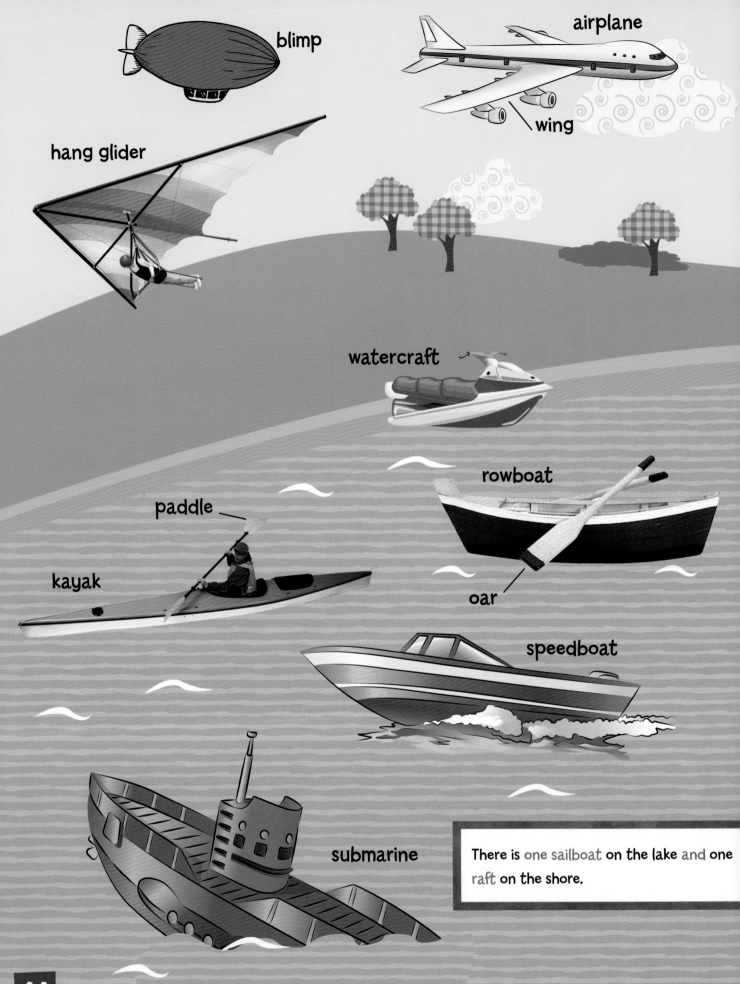

blimp

airplane

wing

hang glider

watercraft

rowboat

paddle

kayak

oar

speedboat

submarine

There is one sailboat on the lake and one raft on the shore.

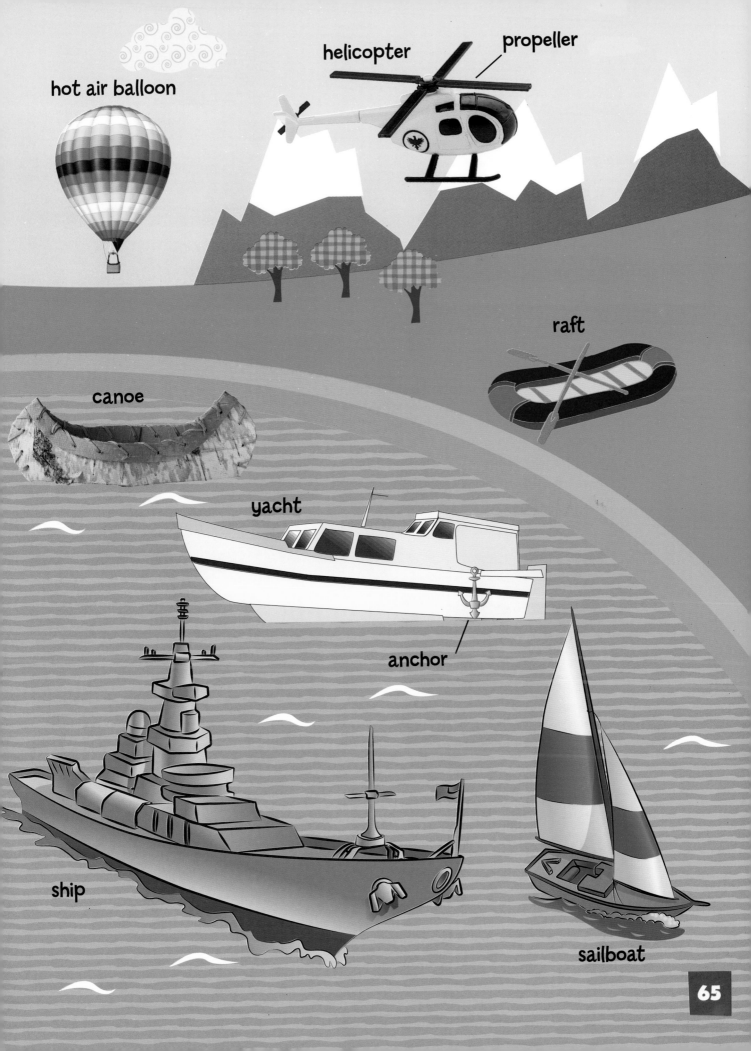

hot air balloon

helicopter

propeller

raft

canoe

yacht

anchor

ship

sailboat

Toys

The **teddy bear** is brown.

The **tricycle** is new.

The **beach ball** is under **the** puppet.

teddy bear

tea set

tricycle

yo-yo

puppet

puzzle

doll

dinosaurs

truck

blocks

beach ball

roller skates

ice skates

train set

jump rope

Costumes

knight

cowboy

fairy

wand

pirate

crown

angel

king

queen

superhero

princess

prince

cape

wizard

Statue of Liberty

genie

mermaid

Music

saxophone

oboe

xylophone

flute

violin

rhythm sticks

cymbal

maracas

drums

keyboard

The top of the drum is round.

The girl played the saxophone again.

cello

trombone

accordion

bongos

tuba

harmonica

trumpet

tambourine

guitar

recorder

piano

71

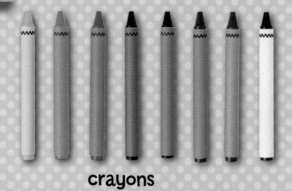

crayons

clay

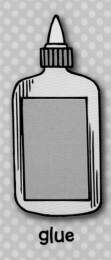

glue

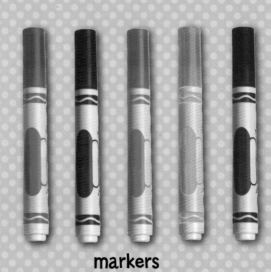

markers

tape

paint

paintbrushes

stapler

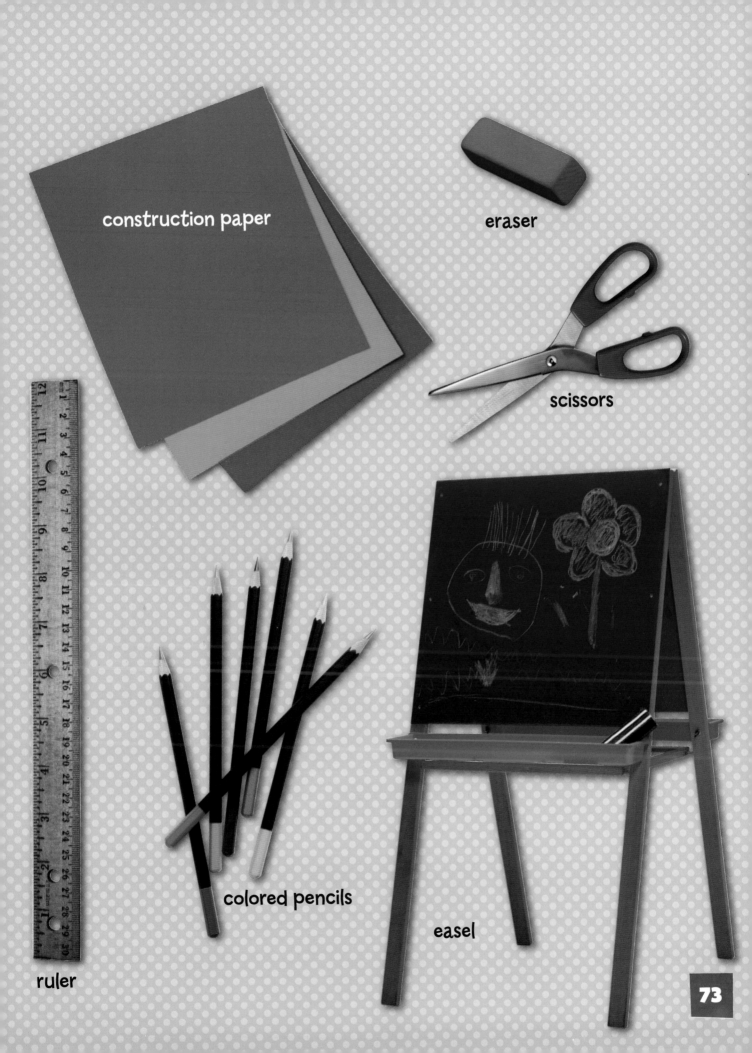

construction paper

eraser

scissors

colored pencils

easel

ruler

Sports

soccer

net

soccer ball

baseball

bat

goggles

swimming

flippers

hockey

ice-skating

hockey skates

hockey stick

puck

74

basketball

backboard

hoop

volleyball

volleyball net

skiing

poles

skis

racket

tennis ball

tennis

Hit the tennis ball with the racket.

Use the flippers to go fast when you are swimming.

The baseball player hits the baseball with his bat.

Solar System

astronaut

space shuttle

You can see Saturn by using a telescope.

Jupiter is the largest planet in our solar system.

Moon

Mars

Jupiter

Earth

Venus

Mercury

Sun

comet

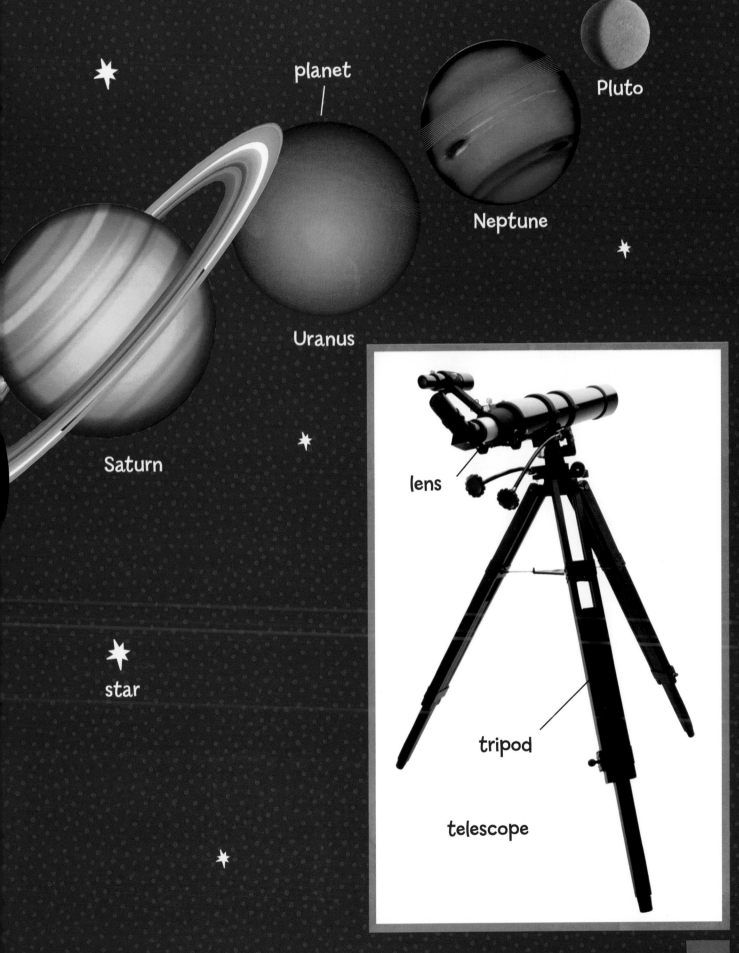

planet

Pluto

Neptune

Uranus

Saturn

star

lens

tripod

telescope

Earth

forest

icebergs

waterfall

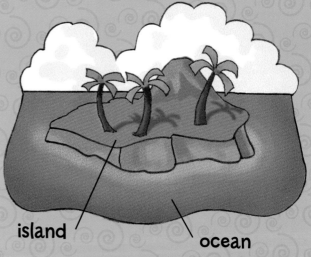

island   ocean

rainforest

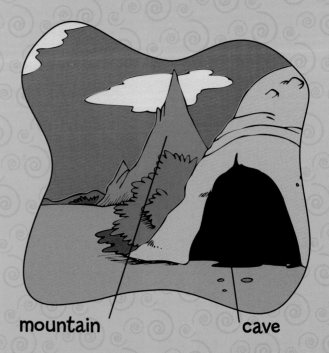

mountain   cave

river

lake

desert

volcano

swamp

beach

Seasons and Weather

spring

summer

fall

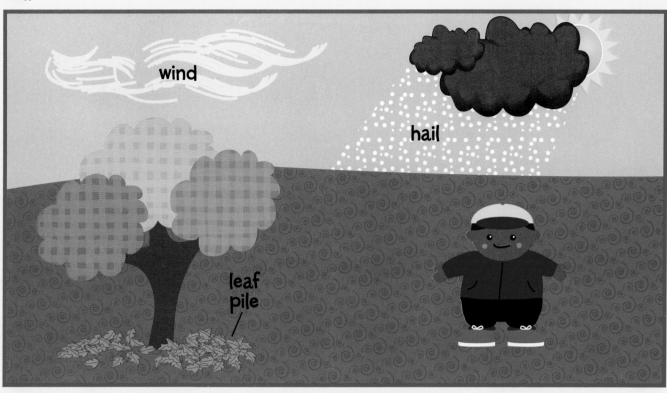

wind

hail

leaf pile

winter

sleet

snow

ice

The rainbow has beautiful colors.

It is cold in winter.

When it rains, there are puddles on the ground.

Colors

blue

white

yellow

black

red

gray

orange

brown

purple

green

pink

Numbers

0
zero

1
one

2
two

3
three

4
four

5
five

6
six

7
seven

8
eight

9
nine

10
ten

11
eleven

12
twelve

13
thirteen

14
fourteen

15
fifteen

16
sixteen

17
seventeen

18
eighteen

19
nineteen

20
twenty

100
one hundred

1,000
one thousand

Money

 penny

 nickel

 dime

 quarter

 dollar

wallet

piggy bank

purse

84

Shapes

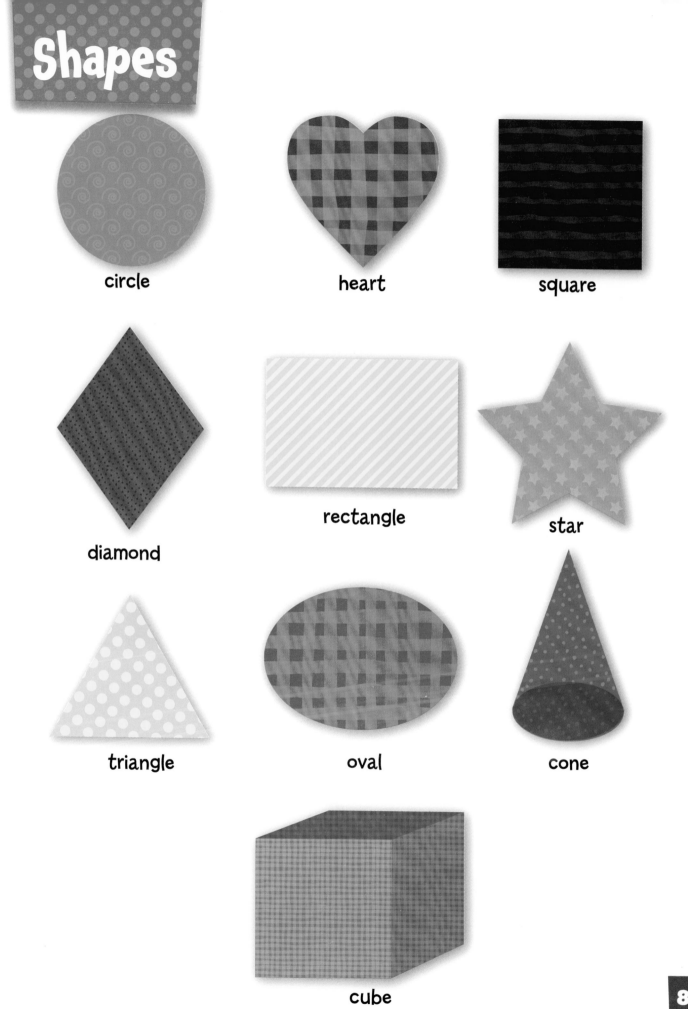

circle

heart

square

diamond

rectangle

star

triangle

oval

cone

cube

Action Words

carrying

building

walking

running

laughing

crying

crawling

sitting

shopping

biking

kicking

swimming

flying

singing

riding

washing

eating

dancing

reading

jumping

sleeping

playing

yawning

painting

Opposites

fast   slow

empty   full

old   new

wet   dry

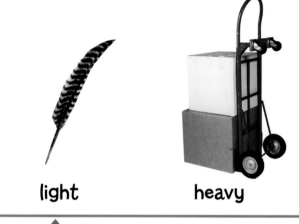
light   heavy

big   little

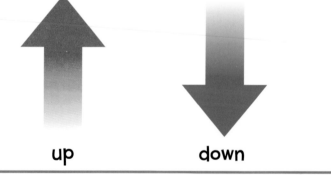
up   down

hot   cold

short   tall

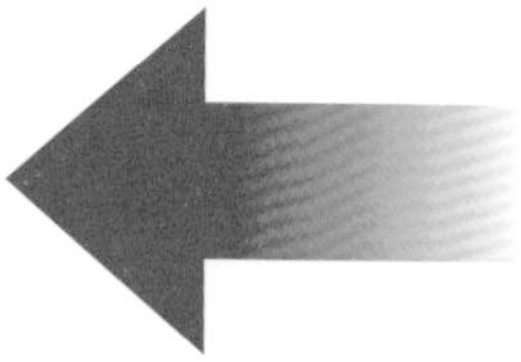

left

right

happy

sad

open

closed

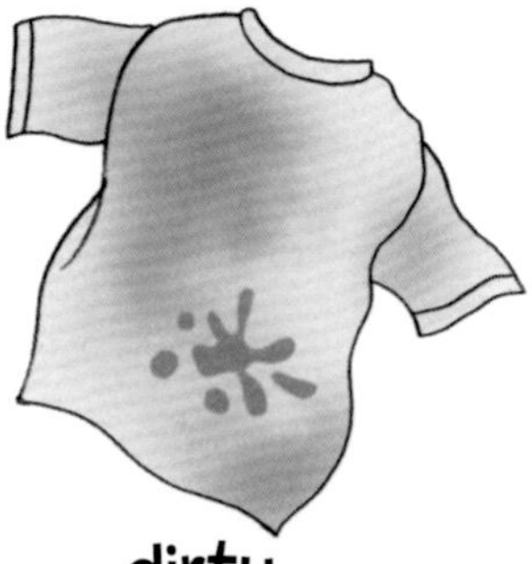

top

bottom

clean

dirty

on

off

out

in

rough

smooth

front

back

soft

hard

Months and Days

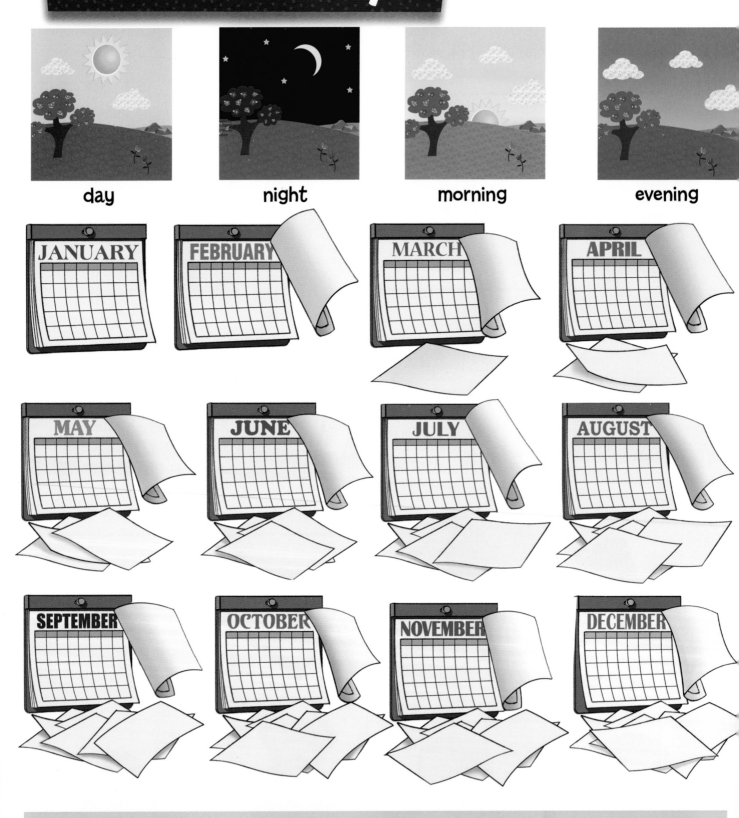

day

night

morning

evening

JANUARY

FEBRUARY

MARCH

APRIL

MAY

JUNE

JULY

AUGUST

SEPTEMBER

OCTOBER

NOVEMBER

DECEMBER

Sunday   Monday   Tuesday   Wednesday   Thursday   Friday   Saturday

Holidays

Yom Kippur

Hanukkah

Independence Day

Christmas

Rosh Hashanah

Ramadan

New Year's Day

St. Patrick's Day

Passover

Columbus Day

Cinco de Mayo

Presidents' Day

Kwanzaa

Valentine's Day

Halloween

Memorial Day

Easter

Thanksgiving

91

Index

croissant, 31
crow, 59
crown, 68
crutches, 29
crying, 86
cube, 85
cucumbers, 31
cup, 14
cupboard, 14
cupcake, 37
curtain, 13
cymbal, 70

D
daffodil, 47
daisy, 47
dancing, 87
daughter, 6
day, 90
day care center, 42
December, 90
deer, 55
deli, 43
dentist, 43
department store, 43
desert, 79
desk, 22
dessert, 15
detergent, 19
diamond, 85
digger, 38
dime, 84
diner, 43
Dinner, 36
dinosaurs, 67
dirt, 21
dirty, 89
dishwasher, 14
diving board, 41
doctor, 29
Doctor, My, 28
dog, 13, 53
doll, 67
dollar, 84
dolphin, 57
donkey, 50
door, 10
dove, 59
down, 88
doughnut, 34
dragonfly, 61
drawer, 17
drawing, 23
dress, 8, 17
dresser, 17
drill, 18

drink, 15
driveway, 10
drug store, 42
drums, 70
dry, 88
dryer, 19
dry-erase board, 22
duck, 51
duckling, 51
dump truck, 38
dustpan, 19

E
eagle, 59
ear, 4
Earth (planet), 76
Earth (regions), 78
easel, 73
Easter, 91
eating, 87
egg, 34
eggplants, 32
eight, 83
eighteen, 83
elbow, 5
elephant, 54
eleven, 83
empty, 88
emu, 59
English muffin, 31
eraser, 73
evening, 90
eye, 4
eyebrow, 5
eyelashes, 5

F
face, 4
fairy, 68
fall, 81
Family, My, 6
farmer, 50
farmhouse, 51
fast, 88
father, 6
faucet, 16
feathers, 58
February, 90
fence, 10
ferret, 53
field, 50
fifteen, 83
fin, 56
finger, 5
fingernail, 5

fire extinguisher, 26
firefighter, 26
fire hydrant, 26
fireplace, 12
fire pole, 26
Fire Station, 26
fire truck, 26
fish (food), 31
fish (animal), 57
five, 83
flag, 22
flamingo, 58
flashlight, 27
flip-flops, 9
flippers, 74
floor, 12
florist, 43
flowers, 21
Flowers, 46
flute, 70
fly, 61
flying, 87
foot, 5
forehead, 5
forest, 78
fork, 15
forklift, 39
four, 83
fourteen, 83
fox, 55
frame, 17
Friday, 90
front, 89
front loader, 39
fruit, 31
full, 88

G
garage (home), 10
garage (mechanic), 42
Garage and Laundry, 18
gardener, 20
garlic, 32
gas station, 42
gate, 10
genie, 69
gills, 56
giraffe, 54
girl, 24
glass, 14
globe, 23
glove, 8
glue, 72
goat, 50
goggles, 74
goldfish, 52

goose, 51
gown, 28
grader, 39
granddaughter, 6
grandfather, 7
grandmother, 7
grandson, 6
grapefruits, 33
grapes, 31
graph, 28
grass, 40
grasshopper, 61
gray, 82
green, 82
green beans, 30
greenhouse, 20
guinea pig, 52
guitar, 71
gum balls, 37

H
hail, 81
hair, 5
hair dryer, 16
Halloween, 91
ham, 31
hamburger, 35
hammer, 18
hamster, 53
hand, 5
hang glider, 64
Hanukkah, 91
happy, 89
hard, 89
hard hat, 38
harmonica, 71
hat, 8
hatchet, 26
hay, 51
head, 5
headlight, 62
heart, 85
heavy, 88
heel, 4
helicopter, 65
helmet, 26
hen, 50
high chair, 14
hip, 4
hockey, 74
hockey skates, 74
hockey stick, 74
Holidays, 91
Home, My, 10
honey, 34
hood, 62